CHRISTLIKE OR CHRISTLESS

For Christians Only

by

Sylvia Bruce

DORRANCE
PUBLISHING CO
EST. 1920
PITTSBURGH, PENNSYLVANIA 15238

The contents of this work, including, but not limited to, the accuracy of events, people, and places depicted; opinions expressed; permission to use previously published materials included; and any advice given or actions advocated are solely the responsibility of the author, who assumes all liability for said work and indemnifies the publisher against any claims stemming from publication of the work.

Dorrance Publishing Co
585 Alpha Drive
Suite 103
Pittsburgh, PA 15238
Visit our website at *www.dorrancebookstore.com*

ISBN: 978-1-4809-3622-5
eISBN: 978-1-4809-3599-0

CHRISTLIKE OR CHRISTLESS

Every penny of this book will be used to serve the Lord
I will not use any for my own personal use. Period
Glorybound
Del Baptist Temple
God's Assembly
Cowboy Church
Baptist Church on N.W. 16 and Meridian could be on 15 or 17 before Meridian.

I will stay at the door until every person that needs to talk or who needs a handshake or a hug has left.

I will give God all the honor, glory and praise.

We as Christians appear to have no fear of God.

When have we knocked on a door to ask them to church?

Left a church tract even without knocking?

Shown kindness in public? A smile speaks in any language!

When a new person comes to our church, do we speak or is the preacher the only one that acknowledges visitors?

Family of God, when have we called one of our family members, of the family of God, just to say, 'I'm thinking about you'?

Are we sincere when we say to anyone, "call me if you need me," then when they have a need you have excuses for not doing what you volunteered for.

We can stay sometimes with people who require constant care so the caregivers have a break.

There are no excuses like I'm not qualified, I don't know how, etc., etc., etc. Jesus was willing to die for you but you do not show the smallest consideration for a family member or neighbor.

Talk is cheap. Get help and organize, you will soon know who will help and excuse givers.

Not everyone has the same talents.

Speaking a foreign language, playing piano, teaching a church class—God has given you special ways to serve him, so pray for God to show you what your spiritual job is.

When we leave for church, do we wave or speak to our neighbors?

If we have not visited them, the *Bible* in your hand says a lot.

Christlike or Christless

Pull the pin. There is no action until you do.

Don't do chores to show off. <u>God Knows</u>.

Volunteer but ask someone to take turns. Yard, trash, nursery, signs—all these are important to help at the church.

If you do this to impress the pastor or anyone else, why waste the time? GOD (AND YOU) KNOWS where your heart is.

<u>Genesis</u> 3 asks, "Are we hiding from God?"

To be Christlike is to always give honor, glory, and praise to our heavenly Father. Jesus did just exactly that!

WHAT BEING CHRISTIAN MEANS TO ME

Integrity.

Honesty.

No gossip.

No judgment of others (God did not give <u>me</u> that job.)

Living the light.

Talk about God—If I don't talk about Jesus, how will others know?

Stand up. Change where you shop if they advocate sin (homosexuality).

In voting, do we elect leaders that are adulterers, thieves, liars, or do we read and pray for guidance from God, or do we worship the evil person instead of our Savior, Jesus Christ, the one that gave His life?

Don't brag even when it is something I want to talk about. Bragging says, "Look at me, my work, my contribution etc." My *Bible* tells me that God's part is 10%. Everything I have, He gave to me. Job, income family…I have nothing without God. Just who do I think I am when I say MY home, MY Family, My money, MY possessions? It belongs to God. HE gives me the Honor of writing a check for tithes. It will all burn in the end.

Christlike means praying in secret (the closet) because God says He will reward you openly. This has been so true in my life. (I would love to tell the stories of God's love for me.) Call me anytime.

Also, tithes mean more than just money. Best secrets get me the reward in so many ways: Time visiting nursing homes, indigents, housebound folks, neighbors etc.

God, please help me to set an example for my kids. The phone rings and we tell the kid to say I am not here. Good job, Mom or Dad, you have just taught your child to lie.

Say to your child, I was wrong, please forgive me.

Read the instructions, pay attention to the roadmap: <u>The Bible, Honesty.</u>

Do I use any excuse not to go to church? (I broke my fingernail, etc.) My family sees me mirror how to live.

Do I visit God's house at every privilege or make excuses?

I wonder if this were my last day on earth, where would I be if this were the day Jesus comes? Would I find an excuse for not going home to be with Him or have I already missed heaven?

<u>Mark</u> 6:17-56 asks whether I will stand up for The Lord or cave in to the idea that sin is okay. When we know wrong is being done to someone else, do we keep silent, because we may lose our job, our income, our home, our family? Jesus paid the price for our sin when he did not owe the debt we could not pay.

When I let sin into my home—family shacking up without the benefit of marriage—sin will grow and grow when I breach the commandments of God. God speaks often of husband and wife, not wife and wife or husband and husband. Dope, alcohol, addictions along with unwanted pregnancy are all examples of sin.

The 10 commandments....

The 10 Commandments....

The 10 Commandments....

When others see me follow them, they know what I believe. Do I believe the *Bible* or not? If not, what is the point in reading the Word of God?

<u>Christlike or Christless.</u>

Playing a musical instrument, teaching, preaching, giving, etc.—are you doing this so you can give God the honor, glory and praise OR is this what you do to be seen? Tithe. After all, how do you pay your bills? With the money coming into your household, income, social security, retirement, etc. Even in the biblical days, the money from tithes and offerings must have surely been used to pay for the tents, labor hire, tabernacle, candle wax, and other needs of the church.

God has given us everything but we use every excuse not to help the church. Would I have anything were it not for God's merciful provision for me?

Money does not get us in heaven nor do works we do to show others. God knows our every thought.

I wonder how many rich people attend a very small, struggling church where their tithes might keep the doors open.

Rather, the big church is full because your boss, lawyer, or doctor are there for the same reason you are. The lawyer goes where the judge goes; he may need to have his help for his client. The nurse goes where the doctor is, etc.

We will find God is always there when these (friends) have no use for us.

A true Christian has no need to boast (I go to church where my boss, friend, lawyer, dentist, etc. goes). The Christian has no need for money, recognition, power.

After all, he has a mansion built on the hilltop that only he and God need to know about.

Do we put our faith in God, man, technology (storm cellars)?

God has always taken care of our every need, providing caves, palm trees to build homes, etc.

How dare we judge a prostitute. Jesus DID NOT.

We have no idea what this person has to live with, and why are we not as harsh with the man? He is participating as well.

Aren't we just that—a prostitute in so many ways? I have a headache, and I'm too tired.

What excuse would we use if we knew we were dying of cancer, or another disease? We don't know now what is in our body (Jesus does).

Would it make a difference in how we think and act before we die? When you see Jesus, will we be given another chance or have we waited too long?

How many times have we taken the time to call the number on a service-vehicle as they passed us on the road with a scripture or other biblical message (Jesus died for you) or something that shows where their heart is? To encourage them by making that call and to thank them for their service to God?

Acts 2:44-47 is an example of taking a verse and not studying the *Bible* yourself as in the Jim Jones suicidal pact. He convinced many of his followers that that is what God wanted them to do. This shows they were following Jim Jones the man, not the Jesus Christ that gave His life for our sins. These verses say, "And all that believed were together and had all things common. And sold their possessions and goods and parted them to all men as every man had need. And they, continuing daily with one accord in the temple and breaking bread from house to house, did eat their meat <u>with gladness and singleness of heart,</u> <u>praising God</u> and having favor with all the people. And the Lord added to the church daily such as should be saved." Commentary is like a person who thinks they are always right. Rain, snow, sleet...they will argue semantics. <u>That is</u> <u>why we need to study the *Bible* ourselves rather than take the synopsis of any-</u> <u>one else.</u> So many places have to hide their *Bible* in very real fear of death, but we have this <u>God bought freedom</u> to go to the church of our choice. Praise His Holy Name!!!!!

How do we treat guests in our home? Do we clique or are they welcomed? Why should church be different? Instead of Ms. Jones sitting in the pew next to Ms. Joy so they can gossip, why not at least speak to the visitor?

Matthew 10:8 says, "Freely you have received. Freely Give." What is the most important book in our home?

We must take the responsibility of being a Christian. Like our precious children—we don't ignore them all week then dust them off to be their parents when we want to. They are the mirror of you. Is this the way you wish they will raise their children? Is God, our heavenly father, proud of us or is He ashamed of the way we treat him? Do we get irritated when someone calls or comes over but later realize that we received the blessing that God sent our way in them?

This book is based on my personal experience, period.

Church=building=inanimate object.

We, the people, are what shows <u>Christlike</u> NOT <u>Christless.</u>

The way we look, act, and speak matters.

Do we welcome <u>every</u> person or are we too busy visiting with others, be-cause after all I haven't seen them in a week.

Are we friendly or aloof? If a person has not been here before, do you sup-pose the reason they don't come back is you?

Yes, I know everyone always has an excuse. The pastor did not shake my hand; I couldn't find the bathroom; offering was taken up; if Jesus were here to take you home today would you be ready or are you still finding an excuse to spend eternity? This is your choice; no one else is to blame.

Dear Jesus, my personal commitment to you and others is to recognize my failures in <u>Christlike.</u>

Every single minute of every day, to give God the honor, glory and praise.

VISUAL, VERBAL, ACTION

Do we sometimes use body language to tell someone they aren't welcome?

Do we give looks to the piano player when he is off-key, too fast, too sluggish? These come from the person who can't carry a tune in a bucket and plays <u>NO</u> instrument, but sure can tell the person nearby how it should be done. This miserable person knows full well that it will get back to the musician playing to God.

Yes, I believe Jesus had a <u>sense of humor</u> like I do.

Don't brag "I did this for the church," "gave to build the church," etc. God knows where your heart is.

The closet—that prayer is just between God and me. He has given me the privilege of signing the check offerings, etc. God has everything, and owns all of my stuff; I Praise God's holy name for the privilege of serving Him, how about you? Just like our work—salary equals work done. Most places <u>of business do not hire someone to do nothing</u>.

<u>God probably doesn't, either.</u> He rewards us immensely so will we stand around waiting and hoping to get to heaven or will we <u>be working toward the kingdom in everything we do and say so that others see Christ in us every day?</u>

Hebrews, 10-25 talks about not forsaking the assembling of ourselves together as the manner of some is; but exhorting one another, and so much the more, as ye see the day approaching.

James, 2-17 says, "even so faith, if it hath not works, is dead." This means being alone.

When my car won't start, faith alone will not make it. I must have a motor.

7

Works without faith will not get me in heaven, no matter how much I give. Jesus will not sell salvation. How about you? Are you for sale? Do you visit big churches to donate but ignore a small one in your neighborhood, that might be able to stay open or win souls if only they had a few dollars of the offering you gave to your church last week?

Numbers, 31, tells us "Moses' tribute to the Lord was to be a small amount." After all they had 36,000 beeves, that God had given them. Oh, so you don't think they came from God? Do you also think the Easter Bunny will bring you a chocolate candy?

Will you share it?

What is the status quo? Is this where God wants us to stay? What does it mean when there is 30 in attendance, but seating capacity for 400?

Mark, 8-23, tells us about a blind man. All things are possible through God. If it is God's will, anything will happen—not our will but God's will. I don't believe, if it were left up to any one of us, we would have never, ever accepted what Jesus Christ gave us freely: his life. We owed a debt we could not pay. He paid the debt he did not owe. Thank you, God, for sending your only Son so I could hope for salvation.

Christlike or Christless.

There are many ways we deceive, like with insurance claims. We think, "Oh well, the insurance paid for it, so we never even pick up the bill to see if we even got the service." We can believe if it came out of our wallet, we would scrutinize the bill very closely.

When we get glasses, we think it is painful, so we go ahead and get new glasses. When it comes to the IRS, are we okay with claiming deductions just because we can and not get caught? A thief is exactly that.

Do I live a life that I want my children to replicate or do I want them to imitate me in everything I do and everything I say?

When you said, "just tell them I am not here," that just taught your child to LIE and we wonder why our child lies to their parents.

It works as well to say, "I will call them back," and then do what you told your child you would do. They are paying attention to everything and children will remember everything you did or said long after you.

When it comes to preachers, are there payment expenses? Are these on the up and up or are you too lazy to ask questions or even care where the money from offerings goes as long as it does not interfere with your pattern? What about God's pattern?

God says the church family is our family. Why is it after we leave church, we don't have the time to call an elderly member but we always have time to call some "important person?"

Praise God; I am important in God's eyes and that is where I will spend eternity.

Do we see ourselves as God sees us and as others see us?

Do we notice the many things we do daily that do not follow the ten commandments?

God gave us commandments, lessons to keep, a roadmap: the BIBLE. It says, "For what it profit a man if he shall gain the whole world and lose his own soul."

Are we so pious that we think the rules are for everyone else but we can do what we want to?

One of the ten commandments talks about Gossip.

Have you noticed we who cannot carry a tune in a bucket are the first to cast stones?

We say, "He was off-key. Too loud, too soft, can't stay in sync." These comments are usually accompanied by that look; I don't like this music, etc.

Christians use some fantastic excuses for not helping at the church or even going to church.

I broke my fingernail, I won't make it. My foot hurts from surgery, etc. That surgery was four months ago—it should be able to do for awhile. The difference between you and the sinner is you are saved by grace so it helps you to know that you actually think you are fooling someone. God knows where we are and how sick we are—probably not too sick to push the remote on the television. The sinners are at least honest; most of them at least don't pretend they believe.

Obligations

Don't think up jobs for others to do, then disappear. We all are equal in the family of God. Just like the jobs at home, someone has to eventually do laundry, dishes, make beds, even when we don't think it is our job.

Luke, 10-2, says, "There said he unto them. The harvest truly is great but the laborers are few. Pray ye, therefore, the Lord of the harvest, that he would send forth laborers into his harvest. These are the words of Our Lord, Jesus Christ."

Being Christlike means not repeating rumors that I don't know are the facts. For instance, Mormons, Catholics, and Pentecostals… I just want to be in heaven with my God, no matter what religion you call me.

Faith without works is dead according to James. No Christian said anywhere in history what we do. Then say I'm saved; go do what's right then everything will be okay.

I believe that Jesus expects more of me than what I want to do.

The devil would like us to think that is all there is to going to heaven, which is exactly opposite of what God says.

Psalms 115 tells us to fear the Lord, trust in the Lord (Verse 11). He is their help and their shield.

Psalms 14 says the fool has said in his heart, "There is no God; they are corrupt; they have done abominable works. There is none that doeth good. The Lord looked down from heaven upon the children of men, to see if there were any that did understand, and seek God."

Matthew, 25, tells us, "the wise and the foolish maidens—they were left because they waited until they ran out of chances."

Do we think of the millions of people that die each day without salvation? What about you? What about me?

Are we really ready when Jesus comes or will we continue to say, "I'm fine." Have we done any very small thing today to give the honor, glory, and praise to our Father, or will we use up all of our chances with lame excuses? Tomorrow never comes for some.

EXCUSES EXCUSES EXCUSES
NO, you wouldn't.

If a children's center, nursing home, school, or whatever—even within walking distance of your home—would you be humane enough to offer any of your precious time, even as little as one small hour a week, to help someone?

The time has been given to us not because of what we did, but because of what Jesus did on the cross.

Just think if every church in our town only took one nursing home each month.

It would not be a burden on anyone if Christians would work with each other, taking turns.

I can do all things through God, who strengthens me.

There are so many ways to bring blessings galore to so many. We are the ones who get the most out of doing for others.

We can visit prisons, orphanages, hospitals, or elderly people at home who are so very lonely. What a privilege we have, to offer comfort to anyone.

I want to be the hands and feet of Jesus, wherever He leads.

Just a "miss you" note from someone means so very much in so many ways.

Christlike or Christless.

A sign is posted at a church reading, "Sunday 10:00 a.m. and 6:00 p.m." but when Christmas falls on Sunday, we close church to spend time with our family. Jesus was born only for us and we close the church of the Lord!

What if people just showed up at the church wanting to ask Jesus in their hearts only to find the sign still there with opening hours but a locked church?

There is no service on other holidays as well: Memorial Day, Fathers Day, or Mothers Day.

Christ died for us but we do not even show Our Savior the reverence of worship on His holy day.

Do we keep in touch even if someone goes to another church, or no longer works at your company?

Church family is just that. After all, if members of our family move out of State, do we forget they ever existed?

WE ARE HYPOCRITES.

We act like we even try to follow the commandments, like do not lie, steal, cheat, or commit adultery.

We can fool most others, but God knows every thought and action.

This book was penned by God; I have the privilege to give my Heavenly Father the honor, glory, and praise through this written word. I am the servant and instrument of almighty God.

Rights are being taken from us each day. Many places in America could not be allowed to go to church. Keep our Bible and say a prayer.

This is not just a fantasy; it is very real.

God sent us so many signs, but we keep living in our sin.

Earthquakes, tornados, floods—do you think that anyone but our heavenly Father has the power to heal the sick, blind, and deaf?

We still have no fear of God.

We need to study the Bible. God has said what will happen.

We seem to have the illusion that we can keep right on sinning, that God is blind, deaf, and unconcerned.

In spite of all the natural disasters, we still stayed in sin.

We think we got away with it one more time, that we are smarter than God almighty.

God made the earth, land, sea, wind, grass, EVERYTHING.

He even created you and me.

When God talks, do we listen, or just let George do it?

Remember yesterday's blessings and tomorrow's hope.

People who have helped us along the way in childbirth.

My sister took me to the grocery store'

That was the hand of God. She had no way of knowing I was in need but for the hand of God.

In Luke, 10-2, Jesus speaks: "Therefore He said unto them, the harvest truly is great, but the laborers are few. Pray ye, therefore, the Lord of the harvest, that He would send forth laborers into His harvest."

Ananias and Sapphira.

In Acts 5, they sold property then both lied to Peter when they kept some of the money because of the belief that they could lie to the Holy Ghost and no one would know. They both died like us; they were given everything but everything was not enough. Their GREED and lack of commitment to God caused their death.

We are so self-consumed we only think of cheating each other or lying, when the truth is so much safer than deceit; we don't fool anyone but ME.

What is our credit score with God?

I want a very high score based on how I serve the Lord when no one but God and me know. Remember the closet.

I can imagine telling mom I stole the cheese, and then her laughter. Mom's gift to me: The Can-Can. She had no emotion but we sensed her caring.

Romans 13-8 says, "Owe no man anything, but to love one another. For he that loveth another hath fulfilled the law."

Men and women think different. God made us that way.

"I can do anything he can or she can." Oh no, you can't.

God made the man the head of the household for a reason.

Women bear the children, nurture, and are caregivers.

First Timothy, 2- 11, says, "let the women learn in silence with all subjection. But I suffer not a woman to teach, nor to usurp authority over the man, but to be in silence."

Here are very specific instructions for all duties, just as in requirements for a deacon or bishop. They must be sober, the husband of one wife of good behavior, apt to teach, and not given to filthy lucre.

Also they must be proved. Deacons' wives must also have very high standards.

First Timothy, 3-5, says, "For if a man know not how to rule his own house, how will he take care of the church of GOD?"

First Corinthians 14-34 Let your women keep silence in the churches; for it is not permitted unto them to speak; but they are commanded to be under obedience, as also saith the law.

1 Corinthians, 14- 35, says, "And if they will learn anything, let them ask their husbands at home; for it is a shame for woman to speak in the church."

Christlike or Christless?

Deuteronomy 4-2 says, "Ye shall not add unto the word which I command you, neither shall ye diminish ought from it, that ye may keep the commandments of the Lord your God, which I command you."

My way of thinking is God wrote the Bible for a guide for us to follow His roadmap.

We have so desecrated God's word.

We have many women preachers who are very knowledgeable in The Bible except to skip over the word if it does not fit with our plans. How sad that not only is it preached but the congregation assumes that if the preacher says, it is a fact. They let others tell them what the Bible says and means, when the whole time all we have to do is read the book—the Holy Bible written by the hand of God.

We are led around (Jim Jones) and we don't even question anything when we know something is amiss. It is so much easier to follow the self-appointed leaders.

The words are taken to mean different things depending on how the word benefits the person using the word.

A preacher is one who preaches.

Prophecy means to predict the future as by divine guidance.

A proselyte is one who has been converted from one religion to another. These are three very different words with very different meanings.

The purpose of any great book educate readers on that subject. The most important book in the whole world is the Bible, and we don't study it so we can learn and adhere to what God expects of us. As we do with our children, we want to teach them so they will also hope to be with us in Heaven.

Contrary to popular belief, Heaven cannot be bought, stolen, borrowed, or received but reached only by accepting Jesus Christ as our personal savior. We cannot fool God; he knows!

He is not make believe. HE IS FOR REAL, THE SAME AS HE WAS YESTERDAY.

God will be the same TODAY, TOMORROW, AND FOREVER. Praise HIS Holy Name.

God, thank you for my salvation!

God provides without fail. If you offer a private plane to send a speaker to New York (bad), you are trying to buy your way to heaven. If your plane is going anyway (good), giving someone a blessing will give you one. God says it; I believe it; that ends my dilemma.

Stop the illusion that we will buy, bribe, coerce, or get salvation any other way but by the blood of Jesus. He gave His all.

Imagine being on that cross.

It may be our responsibility to ask how God's money is being spent, etc. The television preachers can tell us anything; we can't wait to donate for a new jet, home, cars, etc. Jesus had not one luxury, nor did he ever ask for money to hear him speak.

The Lord asks for a mere tithe of ten per cent of what he has blessed us with.

We, however, would much rather not study the Bible, God's WORD. It will not feed and clothe billions of people all over the world if only we are Christlike _NOT_ Christless.

The leader asks and we give.

There is only one way to glory.

CLEANING THE PASTOR'S YARD WON'T GET YOU THERE.

Giving money won't get you there.

Doing good deeds won't get you there.

The appearance of evil sends people to hell.

Everyone does; it is no excuse to not live a righteous life, following in the footsteps of Jesus.

When we become children of God, that says we try not to sin.

No matter who we think we are fooling, there are two of us who knows: God and me.

How hypocritical we have become.

We use any means to get a promotion at work: lie, steal, cheat. We may even get away with it for a while but God knows every thought.

Take good and evil.

My personal goal is to let my children see the Christ in me. I cannot accept the blame down the road when I see the sins I have taught them. How about you?

There are so many ways we totally disregard the word of our Lord.

Churches are used for many things but what they were intended: daycare, games, sports, the selling of merchandise. This is not for the Glory of God but for profit.

Would we open our homes for these uses? But we think nothing of using God's house.

In the words of the song, "If we don't stand up for Jesus, we will fall for anything."

God had his hand on you before you took Him as your savior. Look back today and you will see God was there the whole time, through car wrecks, rape, unwanted pregnancy, illness, and death. Praise God as we look back at the miracles in our lives.

You and only you, with prayer, can change the thoughts and actions of people around you—family, friends, work peers—just by following the greatest commandment: love thy neighbor.

Romans, 13-8, says, "Owe no man anything."

During brain surgery, shouldn't there be pain? With a radium impact, there's no pain ever.

The book is given to me. I'm by God. I have nothing to do with it but to follow the Master's voice. This is such a great honor for me to be given this privilege to pen this for the glory, honor and praise of my Lord.

This book is based on my personal experience as a hypocrite.

I'm forgiven by God's mercy. You can be forgiven, too.

The Bible gives us everything we need.

Give to God <u>first</u>. We forgot where we get these blessings called money to pay our bills; sometimes we think we did it all by ourselves.

<u>Tithe</u>. God asks for only ten per cent of what He gave us. How can we act like we do? God knows.

Tent Makers

Suppose the needles, thread, and other supplies had to be paid for with some form of exchange?

Today

Church utility, electric, gas, phone, and other expenses come from the tithes and offerings.

Do we not have these at our home or business?

Older folk need just a little care and concern. Thank God we have the means and health to be a blessing to someone this day.

Psalms 24-3 says, "Who shall ascend into the hill of the Lord? Or who shall stand in His holy place?"

Psalms 15, verses 1-5, "I fear the Lord. In my awe of God, my goal is to be His servant, by reading and knowing the word of God."

Psalms 24-4 says, "He that hath clean hands and a pure heart, who hath not lifted up His soul to vanity, nor sworn deceitfully."

What that means to me is living <u>Christlike,</u> not <u>Christless</u>. At home, at work, at church, in public—every second of every day. What is important to God is not me bragging about how much I do, how much I give to show off for others. The best blessing ever received is to do things for others that only you and God know about. You don't need to brag about helping the poor. Just do things because God sent you.

Hebrews 13-8 says, "Jesus Christ was the same yesterday, the same today, and the same forever."

How great to have that assurance.

I'm thinking of lost friends, let down by everyone we knew, depressed because they changed. What about you? Were you like Jesus or the world? I know Jesus will never let me down; I have tested him over and over.

I lost years with my cousin because of lack of communication. Imagine a rich man in a little church. There is money in the offering that he gets no recognition for, and maybe he wears holey jeans and worn shoes. Only he and God know what paid the church bills to keep it open.

This is no criticism, just facts. "Tell it like it is."

Regarding halfway Christians, our attitude reflects Jesus to others—how we talk, walk, act, dress, and treat others.

What if God divorces us?

He is the boss. Nobody is pulling the wool over His eyes. No matter how smart you think you are, God created you and knows your every thought and deed.

When there were uninvolved churches, Jesus got involved.

Participate in giveaways, food pantries, school clothes, clothes closets, and food baskets. Be Christlike! It is between you and God.

The biggest deterrent to people coming back to church just might be YOU, the CHRSTIAN MEMBER.

Were the visitors greeted sincerely and warmly and made to feel welcome? Or were we too busy because, after all, we haven't seen Betty since Wednesday night and oh my! The news I have to tell her. There are cliques. Ms. Jones sits right next to the band leader, etc. Excuse me, that is Joe's pew.

The visitors don't have any idea where they are supposed to be, because the preacher was back there somewhere and a visitor had no idea who he was until he stood up to preach the sermon.

In my personal experience at a group luncheon, praise God for Raleigh; he asked someone to ask the blessing on the food with prayer, when several Christians made no move to publicly acknowledge Our Lord and Savior, Jesus Christ.

Tough Love

We are too wimpy with our children, neighbors, church, and friends. If we love God, let everyone know. My thoughts are, there will be no appeals on judgment day. We had too many chances, but we thought we had more time. Although THE BIBLE WRITTEN BY THE HAND OF GOD plainly says, "like a thief in the night, in the twinkling of an eye."

God, please forgive me for how badly I have treated you.

I think of car crashes, heart attacks, sudden disasters, sudden and complete eternity. Where will you be?

The first commandment says there will be no other Gods before me.

God has been replaced with television.

The excuse I use is, "Oh, gee I don't want to spill coffee on my Bible when I am drinking it." So I flip on the television, then after the program is over I have another excuse for not reading God's word, so it is not read, nor will I pray.

Soul winners do what no one else will.

Soul losers do nothing but send people to hell because sinners look at the Christians for an example of <u>CHRISTLIKE</u>.

Someone's idea might be to say, "It is not my fault." They have a choice. This may be true, but if you are the only example of Christian they have ever been exposed to, whose fault is it? The Christian knows God's word. The sinner does not. I fear the wrath of God.

God is such a great God; He gave his only Son for our sins. The word of God is clear that when I disobey my Father, I will remember my sin.

When will we learn?

We can fool everyone, but most of all ourselves, into believing God is deaf, blind, or stupid when God knows our every thought, even how many hairs are on our head.

We should not use God like a spare tire. The only time we think about that spare is when we are flat and in need.

When we take the "I" out of our vocabulary, and put in God, we are rewarded with so many blessings, says Psalms 78.

Even as they were whining, God was providing water and meat for them as He has provided for us every second of every day of our lives. Can we not see the blessings?

Even if the only thing we do is breath, God gave us that breath. God could just as easily take it away, along with homes, children, family, or Money (read Job) to get a clear insight into a just man.

Take homeless people for example. Let's give to God instead of constantly taking, taking, taking.

How do we feel when someone does us like that?

Do we have a stopping place? DOES GOD?

We need to fear God (like parents' punishment).

Read the map—God's Word.

Don't listen to a preacher, teacher, or anyone but the true word of God.

Could it be that is why God made His word available in written form, to be read and studied by you and I and no one else's misinterpretation of THE WORD written by God's own hands?

Know your Bible.

If you don't, you will not know what the word of God is, whether it is the truth or just my opinion.

You have to account for it on judgment day before God, not me.

We are all accountable to God. No one else can do it for us.

Will God accept "So and So said it and I believed it"?

This is like parents knowing when their children lie.

Parents are too lazy to ask the hard questions.

For example, if you know the kid has no money, where did that candy bar come from? If the kid gives an answer, then we, the parent, call the other parent to thank them for sharing their candy.

This will teach honesty to your child; he then knows you care and he won't get away with you, his parent, overlooking bad things, because you don't accept excuses, excuses, excuses. Here is my testimony to Jesus.

I am Christlike Not Christless, in every reflection of my life: family, church work, volunteering. First, at church, work, in the community, etc., I am consistently faithful in even the smallest things, like cleaning toilets, trash, the kitchen, or anything that will give God the honor, glory, and praise—particularly if only God and I know about it.

Don't brag to others about ME, ME, ME, to try to make us look good.

Do I really think it matters to others what I do?

A Pharisee says look at what I do.

A Publican says God, forgive me.

In 2 Corinthians, 5-11, it says, "Knowing therefore the terror of the Lord." Do we totally disregard the written word of God when it is so clear and well written?

Regarding women preachers, 1 Corinthians 14-34 says, "Let your women keep silence in the churches; for it is not permitted unto them to speak; but they are commanded to be under obedience; as also saith the law. And if they will learn anything, let them ask their husbands at home; for it is a shame for women to speak in the church."

This means, to me, exactly what it says as the Bible is written, not as men interpret it to suit themselves. The argument you will often hear is, "This is what God means." No. No. No. I think God says what He means and means what He says. No matter how we (human, earthy folks) change what we think He means, the fact still remains. We are not God and we did not write the Bible.

Romans 13, verse 2, says, "Whosoever therefore resisteth the power RE-SISTS THE ORDINANCE OF GOD, AND THEY THAT RESIST SHALL RECEIVE TO THEMSELVES DAMNATION."

First Timothy, 2-11 and 12, says, "Let the woman learn in silence with all subjection. For I suffer not a woman to teach, nor to usurp authority over man (THE MAN), but to be in silence." This, I believe, was Paul's lesson to Timothy on how he should conduct himself as well as what to expect of the people in the church—those proclaiming to be Christlike, but indeed were false teachers with greedy motives.

That is exactly what we have today in our church.

Will we continue as I did for so many years, living in sin?

Had I died anytime then, I would be in hell today in great torment.

Regarding homosexuality or gay Christians, the Bible very clearly says in the words of Paul, a servant of Jesus Christ, "Homosexuality is an abomination to God. IT IS IN ROMANS 1-21 through 32.

SIN, no matter how we think or change God's word, is what it is. Sin without true repentance will be punished!

Man suffers the loss of God's rewards, not salvation.

Regarding a job that gives you a salary, work, you may not get fired, but you will never be hired when you do nothing but wait for it to happen, i.e. longevity for a Churchgoer or tenure. This also includes promotion, salary increased, benefits, etc. at work.

Go the extra mile for Jesus. He did much more for you!

Reap the blessings waiting for you.

Joke, as the chauffeur for Billy Graham said.

James 2 verse 17 says, "Even so faith, if it hath not works, is dead, being alone. Dead faith is worse than no faith at all."

So many works can be done for Jesus: nursing homes, children's centers, check on your neighbors.

Is NCIS (the television program) taking the place of God in your home? Has the Bible been replaced along with your family, with your ME TIME?

In Revelation 3 verse 15, Jesus said "I know thy works that thou art neither cold nor hot. I would thou weren't COLD OR HOT." Jesus says in verse

16,"then because thou art lukewarm and neither cold nor hot, I will spew thee out of my mouth."

Let George do it, chores for Jesus, church, fellow members etc. Well, George gets tired, too.

Communicate.

Write letters to the country. Be positive! They weren't born knowing what to do. We show them by our lack of interest and inaction—we (the taxpayer who pays the salary of each and every public servant) —in not talking to the politician or writing.

Take for example marijuana in the District of Colombia. This issue got seventy per cent of the yes votes.

Where are the Christlike Christians when Satan took over, standing up for God if that is what they stand for?

If we knew God would come today to take us to heaven <u>OR NOT</u>, would we use the excuses we use for not attending church, reading the Bible, etc.?

Our excuses include: preacher that no one knows, snow, ice, rain, sleet, tornado.

When we had the church flattened by the tornado, would we use that excuse not to have service or would we have church outdoors if Jesus was here?

God knows everything—our lame excuses, our hearts, our menus, our intentions.

<u>Christlike or Christless.</u>

Do we go to the big churches because we get more from them in free stuff? Little churches can barely pay the bills. Many pastors of little churches get NO SALARY at all. They work at full time jobs to support their family while being a full time pastor.

Are we there to serve the Lord or to impress? (Lawyers may want to go where the judges go; after all they stand before that judge in court.) Very prominent people might give their offerings to a big one, when a little church might be kept open if they would come with an offering to God; perhaps no one will ever know their name or title because they come to church for <u>one reason only</u>: to praise God and to give God the honor, glory and praise. NOT MAN! <u>God knows.</u>

If the judge or boss you go to church for moves, would you move also?

I was the worst hypocrite, too. Praise God for sending His only Son, Jesus Christ, to pay for my sins with his blood at Calvary. Christians Must Listen!

Leave the talking to them. Let's help even if all we can do is listen.

We have all had the shut outs, when all we needed was someone to listen. God ALWAYS LISTENS. Do we?

When in church, are we in our own little clique or do we SEE visitors and make them feel welcome in the house of Prayer?

Stand up for Jesus. Bibles bought at a major store are expensive. If I can purchase one at Life Dollar Store for $10.00, they can sell it for that as well.

Greed is based on where we buy. If we don't shop there, they will have competitive prices.

We make scalpers wealthy because we are too lazy to look, listen and GO.

Satan is: computers, television, charging admission to hear a speaker. Jesus did not charge admission.

Jesus heals today and still does NOT CHARGE ADMISSION.

If Jesus came today, would the excuse be, "I can't go to heaven because I have out of town company"?

Reading the Bible is not the same as studying THE WORD.

If I am not focused then surely I am wasting God's time.

We are known by the company we keep. Cussing and visiting bars are sins. Not only are my children watching, but God is always seeing, hearing and recording.

Stand up for Christ. Where were God's people when this happened? Some examples include the Duncan High school teacher, Muslims can pray in school but we can't, passing the Gay Law, openly breaking the 10 Commandments.

People in office have been proven to stand against God.

God is not on a timer.

For example, I read my Bible every day. It is now seven and my hour is over at eight. My Bible is slammed shut at exactly eight. I have just cheated God out of tithes of time.

Two hours and forty minutes at least each day would be dedicated to God. Ten per cent of twenty-four hours equals two hours and forty minutes only.

God gave His all to us including that TIME.

If I died today, am I assured because of how I lived that I will be in heaven with Jesus when I gave up my sin to follow Jesus?

YES.YES.YES. Praise God!

The people that died suddenly yesterday, where are they now?

Were they Christlike or Christless?

God speaks to me in the spirit, not verbally as He did with the apostles.

God told me—I have heard preachers say this, do they mean in the literal sense?

A sense of humor is necessary in every day life; I believe that God has a sense of humor. Elijah, a great man of God—maybe your God is taking a nap, on vacation or whatever. My God is always awake. What a wonderful testimony for Elijah to make.

Perhaps we could light a candle to let sinners put their finger over it. This may be the only way we will know what hell is like.

Imagine the little pain; we can remove our finger from the flame, but if we choose (and YES it is a choice) to go to hell the fire will consume the whole body. The Bible says this will happen for all eternity.

"Study" is not the same as read (in one ear and out the other).

Focus.

First Chronicles 29 and 30 say, "Let the earth know."

In 1999, there was a tornado.

On May 6, 2015 tornado, no one died but one person drowned, but yet we have gotten worse in sin since 1999 when so many died. We didn't change. God gives us so many chances and we still do what we have always done: sin, sin, sin like hypocrites, hypocrites, hypocrites.

The Bible says what it means, but yet we earthlings convolute the meaning. In many ways we say this is what God meant. It is my humble belief that God said what He meant, and that is exactly why He wrote in the Bible. DO NOT ADD TO OR CHANGE ONE TITLE.

Here are some examples: Women in silence—1st Corinthians 14-34-40, 1st Timothy 2- 11 and 12; bishops—1st Timothy 3:1-13; homosexual people, putting people in office by our silence; silence is CONSENT.

When only three people attend church, that means silence in anything is agreeing to whatever.

Regarding politics, tell them what you think. Stand up for God, the Bible and the ten commandments. God wrote them for a reason.

With our children, when we allow them into our home shacking up that says we agree. Even if we did this, Jesus Christ died for my sin so when I accepted

Him as my personal Savior, He washed away all my sins by covering me with his blood. Praise God, I am covered by the blood of Jesus.

This means complete. Go and sin no more. Because of Calvary I became free of my past sin and now can look forward to eternity.

Deuteronomy 12:32 tells us "what thing so ever I command you, observe it, too; thou shalt not add thereto nor diminish from it.

Joshua 1-7 says, "Only be thou strong and very courageous, that thou mayest observe to do according to all the law which Moses, my servant, commanded thee; turn not from it to the right hand or to the left, that thou mayest prosper whithersoever thou goest."

Deuteronomy 28-12 says, "And thou shalt not borrow."

Proverbs 22-16 says, "He that oppresseth the poor, to increase his riches and he that giveth to the rich, shall surely come to want." James 4 4 says, "Ye adulterers and adulteresses, know ye not that the friendship of the world is enmity with God? Whosoever, therefore, will be a friend of the world is the enemy of God."

Setting an example is the only mirror of Christ they may have.

So if they SEE sin in their home (living in sin), this teaches them it is okay.

If I wrote this book it would have the title (FOR CHRISTIANS) ONLY.

When in sin we can't see but if we act like a Christian only when it is convenient for us, that might make us an ATHEIST CHRISTIAN.

Please forgive me for being sharp-tongued. God certainly never set me up to be judge.

Because of my spirituality, I cannot watch, listen, see, feel and not stand up for God.

Given my experience at church and with Christians, I must speak.

Look how we disregard God's word in terms of tithes, offerings etc.

What if on judgment day, God used excuses like "I just don't have the time" or "I just don't have the money."

Remember the landowner who gave the little to the bigger?

Church has become SO politically correct. They don't want to rock the boat regarding their salary, benefits, or prestige. They certainly don't want to preach God's word, especially regarding why people go to hell instead of heaven. After all, they may not want to come back to hear the truth so we do numbers, not facts.

Who stood up for the court clerk who refused to go against the Bible? The school teacher that gave Bibles to HIGH SCHOOL students? The Oklahoma state representative who fought against homosexuality? Her peers stood for SIN instead of Christ.

The Bible says in Matthew 10-08, "Freely ye received. Freely give."

Also, personally, when I die I hope because of my faith and my works, together, I will hear from God, "Thou good and faithful servant!"

I don't hope this because I was neither hot nor cold.

I NEVER KNEW YOU.

The choice is yours only. In the end we have no one to blame but ourselves.

You and only you will be held accountable for your actions!

Read the instructions in the Bible.

Here are some suggestions: go, write, call, or visit the capital. See someone who decides our laws. Write to anyone who makes the law and call someone making the decisions.

GOD LEADS.

We have no excuses.

We have no excuse for not standing up for our belief.

In my humble opinion, the world is not in the shape it is in because we did nothing. The lives of innocent people have been lost.

We did nothing or said nothing because it did not affect us.

After all it happens OVER THERE.

They are killing people OVER THERE.

It's actually happening here in America.

HERE IN AMERICA.

In our town, we watch television. The newscasters do a great job of keeping us informed, yet we know and PAY NO ATTENTION, because it does not affect "ME, ME, ME, I, I, I, MY, MY, MY."

Matthew 15- 7- 9 says, "Ye hypocrites, well did Esaias prophesy of you, saying, this people draweth nigh unto me with their mouth, and honoureth me with their lips; but their heart is far from me. But in vain they do worship me teaching for doctrines the commandments of men."

Matthew, chapter fifteen, verse eighteen and verse nineteen is very clear in our Bible:

"But those things which proceed out of the mouth come forth from the heart, and they defile the man. For out of the heart proceed evil thoughts, murders, adulteries, fornications, thefts, false witness, blasphemies." These are commandments of men, not of God.

Psalms 55-16 says, "As for me, I will call upon God, and the Lord shall save me."

Psalms 55-22 says, "Cast thy burden upon the Lord, and He shall sustain thee; He shall never suffer the righteous to be moved."

First Peter 5-7 says, "Casting all your care upon Him; for He careth for you."

James 1-22 says, "But be ye doers of the word, and not hearers only, deceiving your own selves.

First John 3-18 says, "My little children, let us not love in word, neither in tongue, but in deed and in truth."

Help the church work towards the kingdom of God. Remember to do this for the honor and glory of God, not MAN, the pastor, other church members, or any other reason but to serve our HEAVENLY FATHER.

CHURCH GOERS: speak up if you need help with groceries, etc., because we can't read minds. Maybe we will be able to when we are in heaven. Only God knows.

God's word says if you don't work, you don't eat. Here is what these words mean to me.

Second Peter 3-18 says, "But grow in grace, and in the knowledge of our Lord and savior, Jesus Christ. To Him be glory both now and forever.

AMEN.

When a person says it is between God and me, this is right. We will be held accountable for our sin of knowing it is sin but doing it anyway. Indeed, it is between you and God. No one can take your place on judgment day.

Here is how God takes care of us: Luke 12-24 says, "Consider the ravens.

Luke 12- 21 says, "So is he that layeth up treasure for himself, and is not rich toward God."

Matthew 6-19 says, "Lay not up for yourselves treasures upon earth, where moth and rust doth corrupt, and where thieves break through and steal."

Matthew 6-20 says, "But lay up for yourselves treasures in heaven, where neither moth nor rust doth corrupt, and where thieves do not break through nor steal."

Luke 12-33 says, "Sell that ye have and give alms."

Luke 12-34 says, "For where your treasure is, there will your heart be also."

Luke 12 says, "Praise God for His mercy." He has always provided well for my folks and me. How about you and yours? Can we follow God's written word?

We say we will when we see Jesus, but what about now, as in Luke 22-36 and 37?

Matthew 27:24 says, "When Pilate saw that he could prevail nothing, he took water and washed his hands and said 'I am innocent of the blood of this innocent, just man.'"

It was in Pilate's power to release Jesus but <u>he chose to please the people</u>. <u>Would that be me and you?</u> <u>Christlike or Christless</u>.

Do we <u>think</u> making excuses (Washing our hands) takes away our sin and releases us of crucifying Jesus? The answer is no, no matter how much we wash our hands, the fact remains that we must receive forgiveness.

John 19-24 says, "Obviously the evil soldiers believed the word of God because they said 'let us not rend it that the scripture might be fulfilled.'"

But LIKE US THEY WENT RIGHT AHEAD AND CRUCIFIED OUR JESUS. WILL WE EVER STOP?

For many of us who die without warning, suddenly, we waited too late.

Here is my personal testimony. The doctors told my pastor I would not live through the night. Praise God I was forgiven, because had I died I would now be burning in HELL because I was a hypocrite in every sense of the word.

I did so many things that I knew were sins. I lied, cheated, stole.

From all appearances, I was a Christian. But I was just like the evil soldiers. There is no sin I am not guilty of but praise God today if I die I will be in gloryland with my Jesus.

Looking back over my sixty-seven years life, I am so grateful for God's healing power.

I had cancer at twenty-four and a brain aneurism at sixty-two.

I had a perforated colonostomy at sixty-six and a stroke at twenty-four. I had many other things that God healed me from.

I THANK GOD EVERY DAY THAT HE GAVE ME SO MANY CHANCES.

God gave me the opportunity to raise my beautiful children, when it appeared I had no hope.

<u>These are facts</u>.

John 3-16 says, "For God so loved the world that He gave His only begotten son, that whosoever believeth Him should not perish, but have everlasting life."

How wonderful to know that today I can go to heaven, according to John 9:31-41, Romans 8-18,Luke 22 verse 35 and 36.

But now, I believe that Jesus is saying (like we as parents) that this was an important lesson then (Matthew 10-9 and Mark 6-8). But now you are expected to follow instructions and provide for yourselves.

God provided everything they needed before, as He did for us. Here are some relevant Bible stories: Luke 22, verses 40 and 42; Luke 13 verse 25; Luke 12, verses 56 and 57.

As you can see from this book, I am not a writer, nor a speller nor a good conversationalist. I can only PRAY,_PRAY,_PRAY,_PRAY.

The purpose of this is I pray someone's life will be changed because of this truth.

Are you like me? I once just went along with the crowd. I believed in John 3-16, but not enough to give up my evil ways and accept Christ as my personal savior. Again, I might have died suddenly in a car crash, shooting, heart attack, or any number of other things that we hear about every day when we turn the television or radio on. Did those people die without knowing about Jesus or, perhaps like us, they think they will live forever?

My humble opinion is simply this. God has and is so good to us, that we believe anything the world or Satan tells us. We DO NOT read the Bible, God's word. That you can prove to yourself if you only READ and PRAY, PRAY, PRAY.

We swallow so many of Satan's snares hook, line, and sinker.

For instance, we overlook all sins because it is easier.

Do we think God was joking when he directed the Bible to be written?

When God sent His only SON to die on the cross, do you think you could send your child to take his place?

Here are some examples of how we approve when it is very clearly in these scriptures.

Second Chronicle 7-14 says, "If my people, which are called by my name, shall humble themselves and pray and seek my face, and turn from their wicked ways, then will I hear from heaven, and will forgive their sin and heal their land."

James 4-10 says, "Humble yourselves in the sight of the Lord and He shall lift you up."

Christian people, even some pastors and ministers who know people are living in sin, seem to be reluctant to teach the holy word when they are given the opportunity. My, this must be confusing to a child born with parents with different names.

Regarding homosexuality, Romans 1- 26 says, "For this cause God gave them up unto vile affections; for even their women did change the natural use into that which is against nature."
Christless or Christlike?

Leviticus 18- 22 says, "Thou shalt not lie with mankind, as with womankind. It is abomination." Leviticus 20-13 also says this.

Ephesians 5-12 says, "For it is a shame even to speak of those things which are done of them in secret."

Romans 1-27 says, "And likewise also the men, leaving the natural use of the woman burned in their lust one toward another; men with men, working that which unseemly, and receiving in themselves that recompense of their error, which was met."

Romans 1-32 says, "the judgment of God, that they which commit such things are worthy of death, not only do the same but have pleasure in them that do them."

It seems to me as though the judgment of God only scares me.

The persons who promote and pass laws that says there is no sin in homosexuality have never read the Holy Book. Or perhaps that they will escape hell if they choose?

God, please today forgive me for the many sins I have committed against you, my Lord and savior.

There are so many sins that we have all committed but God says He will forgive any and all sins if we only ask.

Christlike or Christless.
Romans 6-14 says, "For sin shall have no dominion over you for ye are not under the law but under grace."

Praise be to God that we are under GRACE, not the laws that will send people to HELL. We choose Jesus Christ or Hell.

The answer to everything is in the Bible if it is read instead of taking someone else's word.

We seem to be too lazy to even find out if the Bible is factual. Matthew 9-37 says, "Spoken from God to his disciples, the harvest truly is plenteous, but the laborers are few."

I hope some true, Godly person with instructions clear and precise on how to study the Bible and references and scriptures straight from God will write something to give God the honor, glory and praise. It seems to me that every Bible study book has the authors' opinion, but it is far, far, far away from THE HOLY BOOK of our Lord and savior.

We have changed God's law to suit ourselves.

All we need to do to have an easy life here on earth is do what God expects; that is probably why we have this thing called common sense.

If we take only a moment and see our blessings God has given us we would read and know God's Word.

I know I get so confused in reading the Bible. But I also know if I use the common sense God blessed me with when I ask, God shows me in full clarity what He expects of us and the consequences of or laziness on our part. For instance, we shouldn't trust scholars, false television preachers, imitation Christians, but we should praise God. The Bible is written so you and I get it straight from God's own heart. FOR THE SON OF MAN SHALL COME IN THE GLORY OF HIS FATHER WITH HIS ANGELS AND THEN HE SHALL REWARD EVERY MAN ACCORDING TO HIS WORKS. (Genesis 8-22).

God says what He means and means what He says, according to Revelation, chapter twenty-two.

First Timothy 2-5 says, "For there is one God, and one mediator between God and men, the man Jesus Christ!"

Here is what the Bible says about women preachers. 1 Timothy 2-11,12 says, "Let the woman learn in silence with all subjection. But I suffer not a woman to teach, nor to usurp authority over the man, but to be in silence."

Christlike or Christless

I am simply saying that we have taken the HOLY WORD and changed it to fit us.

Other scriptures pertaining to WOMEN are found in THE BIBLE: 1 Corinthians 14-34,35; Deuteronomy 4-2 says it all in one verse: "Ye shall not add unto the word which I command you, neither shall ye diminish ought from it, that ye may keep the commandments of the Lord your God which I command you."

Joshua 1-6 says, "Be strong and of a good courage."

Joshua 1-7 says, "Be thou strong and very courageous."

This is something we lack.

Here is what the Bible says about speaking-in tongues: 1 Corinthians, chapter 14; Acts 2, particularly verses 4, 6, and 8.

Here is what I think it means. Mexicans, Russians, Germans, Japanese, Romans—speaking in tongues means wherever we were born. For instance, if we are born in China that is the language we speak.

Acts 2-8 says we will receive the Holy Ghost, that "whosoever shall call on the name of the Lord shall be saved. Verse twenty-one tells us about how we hear every man in our own tongue, wherein we were born (language).

The reason I wrote this is because I believe that we as Christians (we claim) are sending people to Hell.

Yes, I know we have the choice, however (based on my personal experience of sixty-seven years encountering "Christians") had it not been for God sending someone to me (angels unaware), I would most likely be dead and burning in Hell this very minute.

"And it shall come to pass that whosoever, even me or you, shall call on the name of the Lord shall be saved."

The fact is you will DIE. God gives you that choice to live in agony in HELL.

God, I thank you, I praise your HOLY NAME. I was given the choice. I pray for the folks just like me who thought just like I did, that tomorrow comes. But this is not true for the people burning in HELL this very minute after a car crash or sudden heart attacks.

Regarding atheism, the belief that there is no God—where are they now? Death is very real.

I know that this book will not change your mind but if just one person will turn to God's word (the Bible), if only this saves even one person, it certainly is well worth it.

Soul winners do what no one else will.

Soul losers do nothing but send people to HELL because they (sinners or other people who do not know God) look to YOU for an example of CHRISTLIKE.

I think God will get even when we disobey Him! We will remember our sin.

When will we learn? We can fool everyone, even ourselves, but God knows it all.

We can't use God or God's house for OUR wants. Prioritize.

God is not a spare tire. I don't ever think of my spare until I get a flat. Then I remember I have a spare only when it is needed. When we take the "I" out of our vocabulary and put in God we are
rewarded with so many blessings.

Take, for example, Psalms 78, which says, "Even as Israelites were doing nothing but whine, God still sent them water and meat regularly."

Can we not see the blessings of God every single minute of every day?

Even if the only thing we can do is breathe, God alone gave us that breath.

He could just as easily take that same breath away, just like the many other blessings God gave us: family, children, homes, money, the church. So many places cannot worship, own a BIBLE or have the freedom we take for granted.

Homeless people represent just one way we can serve God. There, but for the grace of God, go I.

Let's give to God instead of constantly taking, taking, taking.

How do you feel when someone does something to you like that? Do you have a stopping place? Does God?

We need to fear God.

CHRISTLIKE OR CHRISTLESS?

Parents, we know the rules and the consequences of ignoring them. We should punish. Read the map—God's word. Don't listen to a teacher, preacher, or any source but the TRUE and reliable source of our very existence: the man, Jesus Christ, sent from God, that gave His very life, dying a horrible death for you and me.

God made His word available in written form, PRAISE HIS HOLY NAME.

We can study God's word. That way, we don't have anyone's opinion.

If we know THE BIBLE we know what is true or just someone's opinion.

You have to account for it before God. No one else can do it for us.

Have we forgotten—at heaven's door will God accept "So and so said it and I believed it but I was too lazy to read the Bible" or "when the church had service, I did not have time to go"? These are excuses. On Judgment day, will I have an excuse? Just as parents know when their kids lie, God knows.

Sometimes parents are too lazy to ask the hard questions, for instance, "where did you get that candy bar?" If your kid knows, you will call the other parent and say thank you. He should know he will not get away with the theft (if that is what it is) because you will not accept anything but the truth.

Here is my testimony for Jesus.

<u>I did my very best.</u>

Here are my reflections for everyone—family, church, work, neighbors—on what being a Christian means to me: doing what I can without trying to show off, particularly if no one but God and I know.

It means being the first to volunteer at church, being consistently faithful in even the very minute things.

It means cleaning church toilets, emptying trash or anything to give God the honor, glory, and praise.

It means not bragging to others to make us look good (does any human really care if you picked the trash up on your way in?).

A pharisee says, "look at me, what I do."

A republican says, "God, please forgive me of my sins."

Man suffers the loss of reward (not their salvation) because they don't do for God what they could, and I believe are called to do so.

This is, to me, like work. You may not get fired because you may have tenure, longevity, etc. But you may not ever go higher in terms of promotion, salary increases, benefits, etc.

Go the extra mile for Jesus and reap the benefits of the blessings God so very freely gives. We who take for granted these gifts from above, that we take credit for.

Do you know the joke about being a chauffeur for Billy Graham?

<u>The book of James</u> says, "Faith without works is dead."

Dead faith is worse than no faith at all. Could this be the CHRISTIAN that almost never goes to his house of worship or the one that does not tithe, even when this is discussed very clearly in the Bible? Just think, God could have just taken ten per cent in taxes, but praise God, He chose to let us make that contribution, but it seems we have too many excuses not to give BACK to God what he asks (a very small ten per cent) when without God, we would not have it.

Perhaps we think WE DID IT ALL BY OURSELVES AND THE PEOPLE WHO HAVE LESS ARE NOT AS SMART AS WE ARE.

God is the way, the truth and the <u>LIGHT</u>.

<u>Here are some examples of works: visiting children's centers, visiting nursing homes, knowing and checking in on neighbors. My</u> prayer is that people will see God in me.

Is NCIS, television, etc., more important than the Bible, God or your family?

Revelation 3:15-16 says, "I know thy works, that thou art neither cold nor hot. So then because thou art lukewarm and neither cold nor hot, I will spew thee out of my mouth."

Let George do it: cleaning the church, giving offerings, etc. Well, George gets tired too.

<u>COMMUNICATE</u>.

We CHRISTIANS sit back and do nothing or say nothing.

Silence means you agree with whatever laws or privileges. If you don't agree or do agree, get involved. Tell them what you want.

Write letters to the leaders of our country. Be positive! The leaders were not born knowing what to do. We show them (we taxpayers who sign their paychecks) what we expect and want them to do by our disinterest and inaction in NOT talking to them or writing to them.

Take for example marijuana in the District of Columbia. Seventy per cent voted for it to be legal. Where were the Christians when Satan took control? Were we standing up for God if we truly believe that this is against God's law?

If a teacher Giving Bibles to HIGH SCHOOLERS, is he in jeopardy of being fired? State Representative Sally Kern (Oklahoma) stated publicly her Bible says homosexuality is an abomination against God. The law was passed for gay marriage.

Where are we, <u>CHRISTLIKE</u> OR <u>CHRISTLESS?</u>

I thank God for these people who stand up.

If we knew God would come today, would we have excuses, excuses, excuses for not being here?

God knows our everything—mind, heart, true intentions.

Do we go to the big churches to impress others? Do lawyers go to be seen by the judges they may need to be in front of?

Doctors might want a title and know where to go to be seen by their peers. Are they hypocrites? If your judge or boss moved to a different locale, would you, too?

Think about if your donation (to impress) went to a small, struggling church that might then be able to keep the doors open. If only there was enough money to pay the bills. It does not need to be known by anyone but

YOU and GOD. Those are the biggest and get the best blessings. Offerings are just between YOU and God.

<u>Christians</u> <u>Must</u> <u>Listen.</u>

We have two ears and one mouth. Leave the talking to them. Let's help if this is all we can do, we can let them talk.

God always listens; <u>DO WE</u>?

When in church are we in a clique or do we see visitors and make them feel welcome?

We appear to be interested only in profit, making people feel good, etc., instead of telling them the truth.

Regarding for-profit retailers, I can buy a Bible at Dollar General for $10.00. The exact Bible is sold for $16.99 at a Christian Book Store. The fact is, if we don't shop there, they will have competitive prices because quite obviously if one store makes a profit, selling the exact same thing for $6.99 more means making quite a hunk more on each item. We make people wealthy because we are too lazy to LOOK, LISTEN, AND GO.

This book is based on my and only my thoughts, led by God. I am not educated, not an author, not a writer, lacking in communication skills, along with many other skills. But I believe this is what God wants me to do to: give Him the honor, glory, and praise.

This is not in any way meant to hurt anyone's feelings or offend any person.

I will continue to TELL IT LIKE IT IS.

Should this book sell, I will not use one single penny for my personal use. Rather, every penny will be used to glorify God.

Satan is computers.

Satan is television.

<u>Jesus did not charge admission.</u>

If Jesus came today, would you use the excuses you use for not going to church, with Jesus? Would you say you have a headache, backache, or BROKEN fingernail?

So many folks in the hospital would love to trade places with you.

Reading the Bible is not the same as studying the word.

If I am not focused, I think I am wasting God's time.

We are known by the company we keep. Don't cuss or be seen coming out of a bar or any other place Jesus would probably not be.

God is not on a timer.

If we Christians) say "I read my Bible every day, okay it is now seven and I will read for an hour, and then promptly shut the Bible at eight, we have just cheated God out of tithes of time. If we did as we should in time tithing, we would give God at least two hours and forty minutes of each day dedicated to God's word and work. Ten per cent of twenty-four hours is two hours and forty minutes. You think that is a lot, but God gave His only son to die on the cross for YOU. Jesus suffered horribly, so willingly for me and for you. If I die today am I assured because of how I lived that I will be in heaven with Jesus?

The people who died before, where are they now? Were they CHRIST-LIKE or <u>CHRISTLESS</u>?

I believe a sense of humor is necessary. Elijah, maybe Your God is taking a nap.

Light a candle! Let sinners put their finger over the flame. This is the only way we will know what hell is like. The big difference is you can jerk your finger from the candle. Imagine the pain.

Your whole body will be consumed by fire and have no way out. To think we alone made the choice between heaven or hell—this is nature's way of telling us to wake up.

In 1999, there was a tornado.

On May 6, 2015, there was another tornado. One person drowned, but no one else died. But it seems we have gotten worse in sinning since the tornado took so many lives in 1999. We did not seem to grasp how fast our lives can be gone (like a thief in the night).

Proverbs 22-16 says, "He that oppresseth the poor to increase his riches, and he that giveth to the rich shall surely come to want."

The Bible has everything there is to learn about anything. For instance, the Bible has love stories, tells us how to act, has history lessons, science, and architecture.

In Biblical concepts, there is no need to guess what God expects of us. He laid it out for us very clearly.

<u>Women</u> are discussed in 1 Corinthians 14:34 through 40 and 1 Timothy 2:11-12.

Bishops are discussed in 1 Timothy 3:1-13.

Parenting and marriage (how to treat husbands as well as how to treat wives) and money management—anything can be found in the Holy Word of God: <u>THE BIBLE</u>.

Deuteronomy 28-12 says, "And thou shalt not borrow."

There are so many wonderful things that had we followed the word of God, it would have kept us out of trouble. This is particularly true of the statement above, thou shalt not borrow.

How many lives have been destroyed for just this one disobedience? Debt is certainly one of the worst (I think) lies Satan tells us and we believe we can't live without mountains of bills.

A great title for this book would be FOR CHRISTIANS ONLY.

God did not set me up to judge. I will tell you honestly and truly. There is absolutely nothing, no sin I have not committed. Praise God, He stopped me from hideous sins that I would now be, at the very least, in prison for all of my life on earth. God not only forgave me but He has continued to bless me each and every day, abundantly.

I can tell you of my experience trying to find a church. That is one of the purposes of this book. If, because of my encounters, perhaps some Christians will realize that sinners aren't likely to come except if the church is giving something away. I think when giveaways are available, it should be asked that winners come to the service before the freebie. Maybe then they may be led to Christ.

Christlike or Christless means setting an example.

When your children start living with someone, is it because you did this? They saw. They learned. They lived.

Churches are politically correct. They don't rock the boat regarding their income, benefits, prestige, etc. When have we heard a sermon on all the things (or even one of them) that I mentioned in this book that we know is a sin?

It's too late—the Bible says neither hot nor cold; I never knew you.

I believe this means we cannot sit on the fence. We decide to follow Jesus or Satan. There is no middle of the road.

What if God used excuses like I do? I just don't have the time; it's too hard. Jesus died for us. That was brutally hard for Jesus.

I don't have a tithe to give. What happened? God gave it to you.

Remember the landowner who gave little to the bigger?

What can we do?

CHRISTIANS

We can write; call; go to your capital; go to Washington; go to Russia, China, Japan, or wherever. God leads.

We "Christians" did or said nothing because it did not affect our lives.

Change banks if yours promotes homosexuality, adultery, theft, or any other form of Satanism.

Turn off television when you hear cussing from the most popular host.

I only want to serve God by reading and following God's word to the very best of my ability. And prayerfully asking myself, 'Am I doing God's will or my (Sylvia's) will.'

A Christian atheist is a hypocrite who goes to church but does not live a Christ-filled life, but tells himself he will be with you in heaven.

Matthew 15:7-9 says, "God says our heart is far from him." We <u>Christians</u> are teaching for doctrines the commandments of <u>MEN</u>.

Psalms 55:22 says, "Cast thy burdens upon the Lord."

James 1:22 says, "But be ye doers of the word and not hearers only, DECEIVING YOUR OWN SELVES."

First John 3:18 reminds us to help the church. Remember to do this for the glory of God, not your pastor, television guru, or any other person or reason. When you die, that is the one thing: no one will be with you. It will be only you and your savior.

"It's between me and God." <u>RIGHT YOU ARE</u>!

Also, churchgoers, let someone know you need food or help.

We cannot read minds.

God says if you don't work, you don't eat.

What that means to me is exactly what it says.

Christians Walk for Jesus.

Knock on doors.

Sing to Jesus.

I wonder how many affluent people have ever visited a little church where no one recognized them, or donated money to a little church anonymously, that only God knew about.

The $100 bill in the offering that wasn't seen until counting time tells you that Jesus was there in the form of a stranger who left angels unaware.

ANGELS UNAWARE.

When have you visited nursing homes, a children's center, etc.? <u>WHY</u>?

There is nothing in it for us, no name recognition, names on plaques, recognition. These are highly overrated anyway. Take for example a senior pastor signing the funeral book. It makes no difference to anyone but the person who signed, Junior, Senior, whatever.

The person for whom he is preaching at the funeral is still just as dead.

You can see blessings coming every minute of the day.

It is not about being right.

It is about going to heaven.

Put Christ before television, which shows feel-good churches that never talk about Jesus or what He did.

I want to send the $1000.00 SEED MONEY that is guaranteed in four months to be fourfold so afterwards, I can call and see where the fourfold is. I am sure I would be told that my faith wasn't big enough or something.

Surely these preachers know that is not in the Bible. But they get people to beg, borrow, or steal hoping for a windfall in return. I do not believe in the many blessings I receive daily or that anything other than God has been so good to me, not because of anything I did, but because Jesus loves me and gave His all.

God created all this.

Do you think it was you?

We seek titles, money, cars, homes, jobs, and positions. Do we follow the Lord or the pastor?

Only salvation gets us in the door of heaven, says Mark 6, 17-56.

Will I stand up for the Lord or cave in to the idea of me keeping my word of honor to OTHERS who want Christians to do exactly what Satan wants?

If I let sin in my home, it grows and grows. For instance, accountability with family—it is not what we say but most definitely what everyone sees in us.

When it comes to morals, respect, dope, alcohol, or illegitimate pregnancy, what people see in us shows everyone what we believe, no matter what our mouth says.

It is not what we eat that defiles us! (Mark 7:20-23)

Do I believe all of the Bible or not? If I believe only what I want to, what is the point of reading? This includes tithes and many other things I have listed.

Please check every scripture I have quoted.

In Jesus, do we see faith or hypocrisy?

Faith means complete, unquestioning belief.

Belief means trust or confidence that certain things are true.

We believe that our car will start.

We believe our washing machine will start.

We believe we will receive a paycheck if we go to work.

To me, humor is different from mocking. I think God gave us a sense of humor to bring joy and laughter into our lives.

Philippians, verses 7-14 of chapter 4, is to me the most and best way to live <u>Christlike</u> not <u>Christless</u>.

I believe that people of many religions will be in heaven: Baptists, Pentecostals, Catholics, Jehovah Witness. But only the individual who takes Jesus as their personal savior, regardless of what religion they claim.

If we will only remove the big "I" out of every sentence, we could change the world. Replace the "look at what *I* do" with a handshake, hug, pat on the back, or just a smile (which translates in any language). Praise be to God. Pray to God, not an empty space. There are no promises, just wait and see what God will do!

God already knows what is now and what will be tomorrow.

Prominent people might think of OUR homes as hovels. The fact is, it is a beauty; it is filled with the love of God, secure, and sufficient.

Why would anyone want fourteen bedrooms, six baths, four garages, etc.? How many people could be fed with just selling one of these material possessions? Let people die of starvation. <u>NO ONE CARES</u>. Could it be jealousy on my part? Hoping it was me with all this stuff? Lottery, lottery, lottery, lottery. I have a joke about the lottery and God's answered prayer; I would love to tell it. Someone told it to me and I thought it was hilarious.

This joke is not mocking, but has a sense of humor. Praise God for giving us a wonderful joy in a joke, laughter, joy, and fun.

<u>CHRISTLIKE OR CHRISTLESS</u>

When has the preacher that talks you out of your money that <u>God</u> blessed you with EVER called you personally and asked about how you felt, or whether you needed food or whatever?

What about the local pastor who stayed after services to walk among the congregation to shake hands, thank you for your support?

Someone in the audience may need a hug today!

Today let's talk about YOU not about me.

Here are some things I think should happen.

Just because we are a church, should we allow God's money to be used to continually pay rent, utility bills, etc.?

Could we ask for labor hours in exchange for churches paying bills?
The Bible says man will eat if he works (by the sweat of his brow).
If man won't work, he won't eat.

The fact is we give because it makes <u>us</u> feel good, especially if we know someone is going to see and tell. The secret closet—I have found it to be so great to go in the closet to pray with just God and me.

Christ or Anti-Christ? They are very charismatic. They tell you what you want to hear. It seems to be very successful at getting you stealing from God. I tell it like it is. The news media seemed to me to be making fun of the television preacher who asked for a jet to feed the hungry kids in India. Because of this pulling on our heartstrings, he received the millions it took to buy this jet in no time from the ordinary people like you and me. I thank God that the news media aired this. I took their comment to mean that an ordinary jet cannot transport food. It was the very best that could be bought. Thank you, news media for telling it like it is. I know that God blesses these people who do your local news. They are such an inspiration to us.

Noah did not use excuses when God told him to build an ark. He kept on keeping on even when he was mocked, laughed at, scorned, etc.

Don't you wonder when the flood came, how the nail claws on the side of the ship begging for the salvation of their babies? God gave us a second chance. I thank God for that every day.

It is not an option for us to decide at the last moment of life.

Ephesians 4:31-32 says, " Let all bitterness and wrath and anger and clamor and evil speaking be put away from you with all malice and be ye kind one to another, tenderhearted, forgiving one another, even as God for Christ's sake hath forgiven you."

Starting this day, let us forget yesterday. Live life righteously forward. Yesterday is gone forever.

First John 1:9 through 2:15 reminds us "How precious is the word." Thank you, Jesus, my savior, my God, my all.

How about we tithe with our time, two hours and forty minutes each day? Do we take the time or use every excuse to lie to God, <u>steal from God</u>, what He has so generously blessed us with?

Are you late to church?

Are you leaving early or not coming at all?

Are you closing church on Jesus's birthday?

Are you closing on Easter when He arose?

Do we close church for a teachers meeting?

Do we close church for a church meeting?

Is there any reason NOT to worship our God?

As we have our rights taken away more and more, there will be a time that we will not have the privilege of a church or owning a Bible. It is already that way in some places HERE IN AMERICA because we did or said nothing to stand up for Christ. Nor did we stand with the CHRISTIANS who stood up just like the apostles did in the days of Jesus.

Take, for instance, the money God has blessed me with. It is His. He just granted me the privilege of signing the check for tithes. I have the distinct privilege of penning this book brought by God's own words spoken to my spirit. Every word written here is on the instruction of God almighty, to give God the honor, glory, and praise. Every single penny that this book brings will not in any way be used for the personal life of Sylvia Bruce.

Rather, every cent will be used for the honor, glory, and praise of Jesus Christ, my personal savior.

I would love to tell you about God's love for you. Let's not talk about ME but about you. If I could this very day shake your hand and pray WITH YOU, I would.

Do you have to leave church because ball practice or anything that takes the place of worshipping God as more important?

We wonder why at sixteen a child needs the help of Dr. Phil to straighten out what you spent the entire life of this child teaching him.

Do we dress casually or do we dress to attend church as a chance to show off? Instead of talking about other religions, talk with them! Invite them to your church and invite yourself to their church. Then follow through. GO.

Deuteronomy 12-32 says, "What thing soever I command you, observe to do it. THOU SHALT NOT ADD THERETO, NOR DIMINISH from it." Joshua 1-7 and Revelation 22-18, 19 says, "Yet in spite of the very clear instruction, we have many versions of the Bible." What is the right one? The one you heard from someone else or the version you read yourself, written by the hand of God? We shall renew our strength in heaven. Hallelujah. Can you imagine that? Not being tired or weary?

We turn our eyes away when officials sin. In fact, we elect them to public office. We justify it by saying we should not judge (theft, adultery, etc.). These are the people who pass our laws that we are to follow. But their misdeeds are never brought to justice.

Have you ever gone out of town to hear a God speaker then to returned home and forgotten the message? It seems there is a lot of money made here. Jesus charged <u>NO ADMISSION</u>. Ephesians 6-7 says, "With good will, doing service as to the lord and not to men."

When a preacher goes to Africa, is it to inspire missions or a vacation?

How God shows us his power but yet we don't believe!

Look at odd things like weather. Only God can do these miraculous things. The temperature today is twenty degrees, but tomorrow it's sixty. There's a tornado today, but sunshine tonight.

You have a ministry.

Perhaps it is in visiting nursing centers, hospitals, or lonely older folks. Maybe you'll visit prisons where someone may just need someone to care enough to just listen when they may need to talk.

"I don't have the time" is an old excuse. Jesus did. People say, "I'm not good at that. Jesus was.

Take the words I, me, and myself out of our vocabulary.

If Jesus came to town today, would you excuse yourself or fight to just be able to touch His garment?

CHRISTLIKE OR CHRISTLESS

Stand up for Jesus or fall for Satan.

Take your Bible to church and follow the words of the scripture instead of taking the word of (highly paid) motivational speakers.

Don't repeat what scripture says until you have studied it yourself.

Jesus lived it! Did He choose? He died for you and me.

But yet, we don't give our Lord time, respect, or reverence.

Will you do something for our Lord today? He died for you.

The truth is that the excuse you are using is not a <u>REASON</u>.

You don't want to. Jesus didn't want to, either.

Family of God.

When have we called our family members just to let them know they are being thought about?

In the words of this young man K.D., "I had nothing to do with it. God did it." HOW ABOUT TEBOW? Now, these men know their Bible and their God and are proud to show their faith.

Compare these two young men to GAY AND PROUD OF IT.

The simple truth is we choose to go to heaven or hell.

God forgives any and all sins. Praise God.

Why are we changing GAY in the dictionary? It is already in there, meaning also homosexual, according to the *Webster's New College Fourth Edition*, published in 1999.

Be honest. How many of us CHRISTIANS follow the Bible?

Do we include tithes; giving; volunteering anytime, anywhere; going to church? Or do we use any excuse not to, like "I have out-of-town company"? Is the special needs class taught by any of you Christians, or only by parents of the children with special needs, because no one else will? A good excuse is I am not qualified, <u>Jesus was</u>. He was qualified to die for you. When we give to beggars, is it from the heart or because it makes us feel good, so we can brag?

Stand up for Jesus or go along with the evil. Jesus stood up for you.

Daniel 3 says, "If you don't kneel to my Gods, you will burn." Is that not what we do now? Kneel before our television preacher, bosses, or neighbors?

Know what to do: study your Bible!

Be a reflection to all who see or hear you that you live for Jesus.

James said it best: Faith without works is dead.

<u>JESUS DIED FOR YOU AND ME</u>.

He will come again. When he does, every knee will bow. Can we be proud or sorry for the way we led our life? THE CHOICE WAS OURS.

Second John discusses false teaching. On February 19, 2014, at age sixty-six, I came to the realization that Jesus was in human flesh.

Are you hot or cold or lukewarm? Read Revelation 3:15-16. The Bible is literal to me. I know God means every word.

I thank you, God, for your sense of humor as well. As in Elijah in 1 Kings, 18-27.

We are tired but rest on our day off. Jesus never takes a day off from us. He is always on the job!

The Bible is like a best-selling book. Today it is <u>recommended</u> by everyone. Tomorrow it is nothing, because someone said so.

Look at the book *A Purpose Driven Life*. Do you think the author cares? He made billions. JESUS CARES! THE LORD NEVER CHANGES.

Ask your pastor the tough question: how can I help? Be sincere, reliable, and on time. JESUS WAS. Our mirror is a reflection to others. Could we do what the Lord did—give our only child to die?

Amos said, "Thus sayeth the Lord."

Are we Christians? The most highly rated television shows feature cussing, fighting, screaming, hitting, etc.

I want the old-fashioned church with a preacher at the door to greet and say good-bye, to visit the sick and grieving. I don't want the associate pastor, the not-for-show senior so-and-so. If you believe any part of the Bible, you know every word is true. Don't take my word for anything, or anyone else's.

Study the word yourself.

This book is based entirely on my personal experience and on Gods instruction. I will obey.

The song "I saw God today" fits my spirit from my heart, which is meant to give God the honor, glory and praise in Jesus's holy name.

A picture of Jesus is so divine.

We can all relate to personal indifference at grocery stores, food shops, etc. We show this same indifference to our Lord.

Paul said to the Philippians, "ONLY YOU HELPED. ONLY YOU COMMUNICATED."

At what point will we stand up for Jesus? He stood up for us when he took our place at Calvary.

If Jesus came today, would we use the excuses we use for not going to worship service? I don't drive at night, my toe hurts, I had surgery (two years ago), I have out-of-town company, I have a sneeze.

Consider the miracles He did just for me. I drove to work for many years on ice, many miles one way. God kept me in the palm of His hand. I never had even one accident. God, thank you.

Consider the miracle He did just for you—the newborn baby in your arms.

You've gotten so many things from heaven above. Dementia, it could be a blessing not a curse, to forget something horrific, perhaps.

There are perks of hierarchy. We need to pay our own way to see the world.

Jesus paid our way so long ago. How many starving people could we feed with just one trip? How many of us said to our boss, "Please, instead of sending me on a trip, please use that money to build a homeless shelter, feed orphans, etc."?

I am ashamed to say I DID NOT SAY IT.

How many buildings or stadiums have you seen with the name of a homeless person that died, cold, hungry, and helpless? None. Stadiums are named for the rich and famous. JESUS DIED FOR THEM ALSO.

Godly men versus church-going men.

Hebrews 13-16 says, "Do good and communicate."

Regarding church, is this from scripture or your idea? I went to a church service that said for an offering of ONLY $800.00, your name would be put on a church parking space. WHOOPEE!

Now everyone will see your name and know you gave at least $800.

John 1- 1-9 is such a meaningful verse to me, as is John 5-14. There is so much not questioned by church-goers, even the Bible. We are YES people!

Much profit is made because the church is used for, I think, ulterior motives. Churches are used for daycare. Books are bought for $15 but sold to members for $25.

Other items are brought to church for sale, which has nothing to do with raising money to keep the church doors open. Yes, I am very opinionated, but I tell it like it is.

Jesus said, "behold thy mother" as He was dying. He was indeed making arrangements for His mother's living after His death.

You shouldn't stop reading after only one verse in Acts 5-10. You need to read the whole chapter. Had I read just this one verse, I would have assumed that Sapphira simply died of a sudden heart attack and was buried by her husband, Ananias. DETAILS, DETAILS, DETAILS.

Read Acts 5:38 through 42.

There is so much great stuff in the Bible.

We say, "if I had only known," but we did know. Everyone dies.

We lie, cheat, steal but use excuse after excuse for our sins. We must start at the house of God. We must keep our mouths shut and listen. As you can tell from this book, I have a problem with doing just that.

Romans 12:21 says, "Be not conformed to the world."